THE SHAPING OF THE U.S. SECURITY ASSISTANCE PROGRAM

I. Introduction

General Issue

The decline of Communism, the reorganization of the Soviet Union, and the reuniting of Germany are changing the way the countries of the world operate. All areas, economic, political, and social, are affected. In addition to these world changes, the United States is significantly changing. The first Democratic president in years has been elected, bringing a sweeping "new covenant" to our system. He is committed to curtailing U.S. deficit spending and intends to do it by making deep, across-the-board spending cuts. The U.S. is also shifting from a foreign policy of containing Communism to more of an international peace-keeper role. Large military forces once used to deter the spread of Communism are no longer necessary, and President Clinton is committed to downsizing the military to save money. Because of these significant changes, the U.S. defense budget is shrinking and federal programs are being cut. In addition, the new administration has promised to improve domestic stability; therefore, programs dealing with foreign policy matters are especially vulnerable to change. A federal operation sure to be affected is the U.S. Security Assistance Program, which is one of the government's major foreign policy programs.

Research Question

This thesis will answer the question, What factors shape the direction of the U.S. Security Assistance Program?

Background

Security assistance is the transfer of military equipment, training, services, and support from the United States to recipient countries (25: 267-290). Hovey agrees "it is a program that provides military equipment and weapons and training to allied and friendly nations" (19: v-vi). The Departments of State and Defense formally divide security assistance into five programs: Foreign Military Financing (FMF), the Economic Support Fund (ESF), International Military Education and Training (IMET), Peacekeeping Operations (PKO), and the Nonproliferation and Disarmament Fund (4: 3).

FMF is a grant and low interest loan program designed to enable selected friends and allies of the U.S. to acquire U.S. defense articles and services (4: 3). The ESF provides grants and loans to countries where the U.S. has a special security interest to help the balance-of-payments and ease capital shortfalls. IMET is a grant program that enables the U.S. to provide training and education support to foreign military personnel (25: 267-290). PKO provides funding to friendly countries and international organizations which are pursuing U.S. national security interests. The Nonproliferation and Disarmament Fund is a new element in the proposed FY 1994 Security Assistance Program dedicated to reduce the proliferation of weapons of mass destruction (4: 3-4). Because it originated beyond 1988, the Nonproliferation and Disarmament Fund is excluded from this study.

Scope

This research follows the Security Assistance Program from its inception in 1947 through the end of the Reagan Administration in 1988. Specifically, this thesis will investigate the events surrounding the following key events in the development of security assistance:

(1) Greek-Turkish Aid Bill of 1947

(2) Mutual Defense Act of 1949

(3) Mutual Security Act of 1954

(4) Foreign Assistance Act of 1961

(5) Foreign Military Sales Act of 1968

(6) International Security Assistance and
Arms Export Control Act of 1976

(7) International Security Assistance Act of 1979

(8) The Reagan Administration Policies

The research focuses only on the above events for two reasons. One, these are the key legislative enactments in the history of the Security Assistance Program; and two, the amount of time available to conduct research prevented looking at all foreign policy legislation.

Overview

This thesis consists of four chapters. Chapter one is the introduction. Chapter two will describe the methodology used to perform the research. Chapter three is a literature review. Chapter four will contain an analysis of the research.

II. Methodology

This chapter describes the methodology used in researching this thesis. The study uses an extensive, ex post facto literature review. The ex post facto design allows no control over the information gathered and the researchers can only report what has happened (5: 141). This design is appropriate in striving to reach an unbiased answer to the principal research question; "What factors have shaped the direction of the Security Assistance Program?"

The data used to answer the research question came from the following sources: The Dayton & Montgomery County Public Library; The University of Dayton Library; The Defense Institute of Security Assistance Management (DISAM) Library; The Wright State University Library; and The Air Force Institute of Technology (AFIT) Library.

Furthermore, the research findings gathered from these institutions were taken specifically from the annual *Congressional Presentation for Security Assistance Program* reports, *Executive Hearings of the Committee on International Relations*; *United States Department of State Bulletins*; *Foreign Relations of the United States* documents, major policy speeches from key political figures such as the President, and various books, articles, and journals.

These sources were chosen because they contained detailed information on world events, specific budget figures, viewpoints of the current administration, and pertinent background material.

After collecting the data from the sources, the researchers examined the findings, found the factors common to each act, and compared the factors to answer the research question.

In summary, this chapter outlined the methodology used for this study. It listed the sources used to perform the research and explained how the researchers compared key legislative acts to answer the research question, What are the main factors that have shaped the direction of the U.S. Security Assistance Program?

III. Literature Review

Introduction

This chapter covers the literature review conducted to answer the research question, "What are the main factors that have shaped the U.S. Security Assistance Program?" The chapter is divided into three sections: 1) an introduction to the sources investigated, 2) a comprehensive, historical review of the major legislative acts involving security assistance, and 3) a conclusion.

Review

Greek-Turkish Aid Bill. The origin of the Security Assistance Program traces back to the Greek-Turkish Aid bill of 1947. This legislation marked one of the first major commitments of military and economic aid by the United States to a foreign country (16: 183). In 1947, the world was still recovering from the impact of World War II. Post-war Europe was devastated both physically and economically. The Soviet Union was pushing hard to expand its geographic holdings and to spread the principles of Communism. There was great concern that the Soviets wished to gain footholds in Greece and Turkey.

Russian activities in this part of the world had been a concern of the State Department for many years. In 1942, the British and Russians made an agreement with the Iranian government which allowed both countries to keep troops in Iran for a period ending six months after the end of the hostilities of World War II (28: 93). However, when the agreed upon date arrived, the Soviets were actually adding to their forces rather than preparing for a withdrawal. At the same time, the Soviets had been pressuring the Turkish government for territorial concessions. The Turks had been successful in their resistance of Soviet expansion, but if the Soviet Union gained a foothold in Iran, it would become much more difficult to maintain Turkey's sovereignty (28: 95).

Turkey had long been a strategic objective of the Soviet Union. The early czars had tried to gain control of this vital area that blocked Russia's escape into the Mediterranean Sea (28: 96). In July of 1946, the Russians made an open attempt to obtain control of Turkey. Moscow sent a telegram to the Turkish capital proposing a new common ownership for the Dardanelles which would exclude all nations except for the Black Sea powers (28: 96). In other words, both the United States and the British government would be excluded from any future agreements. This would leave the Turkish government to face three Communist states: Bulgaria, Romania, and the Soviet Union. Upon request from the Turkish government and after a careful study of the situation and its implications, President Truman received a unanimous recommendation from the State, War, and Navy Departments to take a strong position on the matter (28: 97). The Turkish government, bolstered by the American support, rejected the Russians' advances and continued to ward off Soviet expansion. Turkey's continued resistance eventually drained their country's economic resources. Toward the end of 1946, the U.S. ambassador in Turkey wrote, "Turkey will not be able to maintain indefinitely a defensive posture against the Soviet Union. The burden is too great for the nation's economy to carry much longer" (28: 98). This assessment was validated by the U.S. Ambassador to Russia. In a January, 1947, report, Ambassador Bedell Smith wrote that he believed Russia would continue to pressure Turkey and seek concessions unless some type of long-term assistance were made available from the United States and England (28: 98).

While Turkey's problems were a result of Russia's post-war efforts to expand, the situation in Greece dated back to the occupation during WWII. Greece and its people suffered severely during the war and resistance to the occupation had polarized the country into two main groups. One of these groups was still loyal to the exiled Greek king and the other controlled by Communists. In 1944, the last of the occupying forces withdrew and the British government sent in 40,000 troops to help in the restoration effort (28: 98). Some of the first questions raised regarding outside intervention in Greece were posed by the Soviet Union. In January, 1946, the General Assembly received a letter from the chairman of the Soviet Delegation to the Assembly which charged that the presence of British troops in Greece represented interference in that country's internal affairs (7: 753).

In addition, the Ukrainian S. S. R. also filed complaints citing incidents along the Greek-Albanian frontier that they felt were provoked by the Greek armed forces (7: 753). The United States representative to the Security Council proposed that a commission be established to investigate the problems. This proposal was unanimously favored with the exception of a negative vote from the Union of Soviet Socialist Republics. The Communist faction thrived on the post-war chaos, and Russia was now openly supporting the Communist guerrillas. Intelligence reports received during this time confirmed the United States' suspicions regarding the Soviets' interest in Greece. The reports indicated that, under Soviet direction, Yugoslavia, Bulgaria, and Albania were attempting to establish a

Communist Greece (28: 98). If the Soviets came to power in Greece and persuaded Turkey to give up control of the Strait of Dardanelles, they could dominate the northeastern Mediterranean and possibly the vital sea lane through the Suez Canal in Egypt (6: 771). Conditions in Greece continued to deteriorate. In a February 20, 1947 top secret telegram, U.S. Ambassador MacVeagh in Greece wrote to the Secretary of State,

> We feel that the situation here is so critical that no time should be lost in applying any remedial measures, even if only of a temporary character, within the possibilities of the United States and United Kingdom. It is impossible to say how soon collapse may be anticipated, but we believe that to regard it as anything but imminent would be highly unsafe (8: 28-29).

The subsequent top secret memo from the Under Secretary of State, Dean Acheson, to the Secretary of State reflected the mood of the time and the main reasoning behind the push for U.S. involvement:

> Reports from MacVeagh and others in Athens are unanimous in their alarm over the probability that Greece will be unable to maintain her independence. Morale of the ill-equipped Greek army is low and areas under the control of guerrillas are increasing. Greece is the only Balkan country remaining oriented toward the Western democracies. Unless urgent and immediate support is given to Greece, it seems probable that the Greek government will be overthrown and a totalitarian regime of the extreme left will come to power (8: 29-30).

Previously, it had been informally agreed that Great Britain would be responsible for equipping the Greek armed forces while U.S. assistance would be confined to economic and financial areas (8: 31). However, in February, 1947, the financially strapped British government announced that it could no longer provide military and economic support to Greece and

Turkey (19: 4). In late February, Under Secretary Acheson presented the findings of a study on the growing problem in Greece that confirmed President Truman's own conclusions. The findings of the United Nations mission indicated that action must be taken or Greece would fall to the Communists. The alternative was to lose Greece and allow the further expansion of the Iron Curtain across the eastern Mediterranean. Also, if Greece was lost, Turkey would be a virtual island surrounded by a sea of Communism (28: 100).

President Truman felt that the ideals and traditions of our nation required us to answer Greece's and Turkey's calls for help and wanted to let the whole world know that the U.S. would not tolerate such blatant totalitarianism. To complicate matters, President Truman also had to deal with the fact that Congress was no longer controlled by the Democratic party. He realized that since his party no longer held the majority, he might have a difficult time convincing Congress to obligate the U.S. to any sort of outside aid program (28: 101-103). Truman placed the subject before his Cabinet and asked for their recommendations on the best way to approach the matter. The Cabinet members recommended a committee be formed to make recommendations to the President. Truman also met with Congressional leaders to gain their support/approval for the plan. This proved to be a key political move and the President received no opposition from the leaders to what he thought had to be done (28: 105). On March 12, 1947, in an effort to signal U.S. resolve in limiting Soviet expansion, President Truman recommended, in a joint session of Congress, the United States provide immediate support (19: 5). President Truman's statement of policy became known as the Truman Doctrine and has been called the turning point in America's foreign policy.

This policy, which included the provisions of the Greek-Turkish Aid Bill, did not clearly delineate between military and economic assistance. It is believed that this was done to avoid the appearance of direct conflict with the Soviet Union (19: 5). The Truman Doctrine was not immediately passed and received some initial criticism. Congress scrutinized the bill thoroughly for over two months. Critics felt that the United States was interfering in the internal affairs of other countries, appearing too anti-Soviet, and making proposals for aid that were much too costly (19: 5). Finally, the Senate approved the legislation on April 22, 1947 and the House voted in favor of the bill 287 to 107 in early May. President Truman signed the bill on May 22. 1947 (28: 108).

The bill provided an initial appropriation of $400 million in 1947 and an additional appropriation of $225 million (19: 5). Of this, $345.3 million was to be for military assistance in Greece and $152.5 million for military assistance to Turkey. The remainder of the funds was used for economic aid (19: 5). The United States also sent military missions to Turkey and Greece to bolster the governments' resolve to fend off Soviet expansion.

The Truman Doctrine and its provisions for aid to Greece and Turkey marked a significant change in the foreign policy practices of the United States. By 1949, the U.S. had increased the size of its military mission in Greece to 527 personnel and, in Turkey, the figure had risen to 410 (19: 6). This was a radical change from the policies of isolationism that followed the first World War. This doctrine marked the beginning of the United States' policy of Soviet containment.

In his speech to Congress, President Truman said, "The free peoples of the world look to us for support in maintaining their freedoms. If we falter in our leadership, we may endanger the peace of the world and we shall surely endanger the welfare of our own nation" (28: 106). The worldwide concern over Soviet expansion and the spread of Communism clearly heightened the ability of President Truman to initiate foreign assistance to Greece and Turkey. This new policy of containment would continue to be the driving force behind the United States' Security Assistance Program.

Mutual Defense Act of 1949. The United States initiated the first key legislative event, the Greek-Turkish Aid Bill, but it was the British that led the way to the second major legislative event, the Mutual Defense Act of 1949.

On January 22, 1948, Foreign Minister Bevin addressed the House of Commons proposing unification of western Europe. Considering the chaotic post-war conditions of Europe, the U.S. State Department welcomed the proposal and the European initiative in forming a western union. Three months later, the proposal led representatives of the United Kingdom, France, Belgium, the Netherlands, and Luxembourg to sign a 50-year treaty of collective military aid and economic and social cooperation (18: 43).

The U.S. followed this lead by developing its own initial assistance legislation policy. President Truman strongly addressed Congress, stating, "I am sure that the determination of the free countries of Europe to protect themselves will be matched by an equal determination on our part to help them do so" (18: 43). This persuaded Congress to approve the Foreign

Assistance Act of 1948 which proposed "association of the United States, by constitutional process, with such regional and other collective arrangements as are based on continuous and effective self-help and mutual aid" (18: 44).

This initial move plus many additional meetings and conferences in the next several months led to representatives of Belgium, Canada, Denmark, France, Iceland, Italy, Luxembourg, the Netherlands, Norway, Portugal, the United Kingdom, and the United States to sign the North Atlantic Treaty in Washington, D.C. on April 4, 1949 (18: 44). It was the North Atlantic Treaty which established NATO, the North Atlantic Treaty Organization. The creation of NATO provided the impetus for the second benchmark legislation, the Mutual Defense Assistance Act of 1949.

How did the North Atlantic Treaty encourage the passage of the Act? Under the treaty, the nations committed themselves to consider an "armed attack against one to be an attack against them all" (16: 6). By joining, the U.S. demonstrated it would be an active agent for creating stability in the world wherever its vital national interests were at risk (16: 7). Bearing this commitment in mind, U.S. leaders realized they needed to start planning provisions to contribute to NATO. They needed the authorizations and appropriations from the American people so the U.S. could provide assistance. Consequently, U.S. leaders created a major program of military assistance, the Mutual Defense Assistance Act of 1949.

The Mutual Defense Assistance Act of 1949 gave the United States authority to provide substantial military assistance to NATO countries. It gave funds to Greece and Turkey to maintain their independence, and to Iran, Korea, and the Philippines to sustain U.S. security interests in those areas.

In regard to NATO, the act established a Council and a Defense Committee which would develop common defense plans for the North Atlantic area. It authorized an appropriation of $500,000,000 for the purposes of assisting the North Atlantic Treaty nations through June 30, 1950. In addition, the President was given authority to enter into contracts for the procurement and furnishing of assistance to North Atlantic Treaty countries in an amount not exceeding $500,000,000 (18: 28-29).

This aid was timely considering the conditions of the time. After the end of World War II, world affairs were in disarray and uncertainty was prevalent in many countries. While the United States and the European nations had drawn down their military forces, the Soviet Union adopted the policy of increasing its military strength through manpower, economics, and training. The Soviet Union consistently maintained the largest military force in the postwar world, with over 5,000,000 men under arms. It increased its military budget for 1949 by 19 percent over that of 1948. The troops of the Soviet Union were estimated to be in better condition than at any time since the war. It had increased its security measures along its borders and the borders of its satellites. And, the Soviet force in Germany was increased from 70,000 to 100,000 men (26: 25). In addition to increasing their forces, the Soviets had formed an alliance, the Council for Economic Mutual Assistance, on January 25, 1949 with Bulgaria, Czechoslovakia, Hungary, Rumania, and Poland (18: 44). The countries favoring democracy perceived this alliance and the strength of the Soviet Union as a threat.

This build-up of force was especially relevant considering the Soviets' behavior just a year earlier. In late June of 1948, Soviet troops and their East German allies placed a complete blockade on all over-land traffic between Western Europe and West Berlin. They intended to force U.S., British, and French occupation forces out of the city (1: 153). The blockade failed because of the highly successful Berlin Airlift, yet it highlighted the Soviet's willingness to exploit any potential European or Western weakness (16: 6).

Besides interfering in Europe, communist forces were on the move in China and Korea in 1949. When China fell to Mao Tse-tung in late 1949, Communist forces and the flight of Chiang Kai-shek's Nationalist forces to Taiwan concerned U.S. policymakers about the security of other non-Communist states in the region (16: 8).

Furthermore, the act authorized the continuation of assistance to Greece and Turkey in the amount of $211,370,000 under the original Greek-Turkish Assistance Act of 1947 and furnished $27,640,000 for assistance to Iran. the Republic of Korea, and the Republic of the Philippines through June 30, 1950 (26: 29-30). This assistance was vital to U.S. security interests because it gained access for U.S. forces and provided a means for deterrence and conflict management. Assistance was given in three forms: material. technical assistance, and manufacturing/tooling.

Since many of the recipient nations currently were equipped with American arms, the countries needed repair parts and accessories. The act authorized the transfer of such materials. Secondly, the repair, overhaul, and modernization of military equipment is highly specialized. The act insured the United States' technical know-how was made available to the foreign nations. Finally, the program realized the furnishing of certain machine tools and materials were essential to enable the recipient nations themselves to repair, overhaul, or produce certain necessary items.

Therefore, it provided military assistance in the form of manufacturing and tooling capabilities (26: 5). The authorization for assistance to Korea turned out to be fortunate because the forces from Communist North Korea invaded South Korea in June of 1950 (16: 8).

Although the Mutual Defense Assistance Act of 1949 made several other authorizations concerning such things as factories, technical expert assistance, and administration matters, the authorizations concerning the countries of NATO. Greece and Turkey, and the region around China and Korea were the significant events of the time that shaped this second major legislative act.

Mutual Security Act of 1954. Significant world events had occurred since the Communists attacked Korea in 1950. These events influenced the creation of the third major legislative benchmark, the Mutual Security Act of 1954. The events included the decline of Soviet influence, changes in leadership in both the U.S. and Moscow, and the resolution of two major world problems.

First, the decline of the Soviet influence impacted the 1954 act. As a consequence of the vigorous initiative of the United States, the spread of Communism had been prevented except in Czechoslovakia, where the government had been weak from the start because it contained Communists, and in China, where the will and capacity to resist had been lost (15: 526).

In Korea, the Communists had been pushed back to their original positions in the north. In other parts of the world, especially Europe, the free nations had been strengthened and had drawn closer together in their efforts to fight Communism (15: 526). While the Soviet influence was declining,

U.S. nuclear weapons stockpiles were growing and the U.S. had 400 stratojets to deliver them (32: 400). Thus, during the first half of 1953, Soviet pressures were somewhat reduced.

This dramatic turning coincided roughly with the advent of new leadership in Washington and Moscow. The Republicans won the Presidency in 1952, the first change in political administration in the United States in 20 years (32: 400). Likewise, there was new leadership in the Soviet Union following Stalin's death in early March 1953 (15: 527).

The new American President brought sweeping changes to the military. With less threat from the Soviets, leaders of Eisenhower's Administration believed the U.S. must curb military spending. Accordingly, in his report to Congress on the Mutual Security Program in September 1953. President Eisenhower made it clear that an additional strain was not to be imposed on the American economy for defense purposes (15: 530). While President Truman had estimated the defense budget for 1954 would be about $46.3 billion. Eisenhower limited it to $41.2 billion (32: 400).

Under the President's directions to curtail spending, Congress also began to look closer at foreign policy. Many in Congress believed the foreign assistance program was escaping from congressional control through the piling up of unexpended balances, the authorizing of "unvouchered" and "no-year" funds, the expansion of transfer authorities, the waiving of congressional-imposed conditions for the receipt of assistance, and other concessions to executive flexibility, discretion, and confidentiality. John Sparkman, a Senator from Alabama wrote, "Even strong supporters of foreign aid had become more than a little disgusted with what seemed to be the self-perpetuating activities of the ever-growing foreign assistance bureaucracy" (15: vii).

Defending foreign aid, Harold E. Stassen, Director, Foreign Operations Administration, explained to the Committee on Foreign Affairs that unexpended balances were unavoidable and actually beneficial. Stassen used Spain and Turkey as examples.

When the U.S. determined a few squadrons of Spanish jet fighters were needed to develop the U.S. program in Spain, Foreign Operations asked Congress for the authorization for money to build the squadrons. But once Congress authorized the funds, Foreign Operations did not immediately use all the funds. The Foreign Operations Administration had to first recruit pilots, conduct pilot training, lengthen airfields, establish training centers, train mechanics, and establish repair facilities. These tasks took years to complete and each of these stages had to be completed before jet aircraft were ordered, manufactured, and delivered. Consequently, the money requested to build Spain's force was still unexpended at least four years into creating the program (15: 503).

Stassen went on to say that having the money up front actually is beneficial to the U.S. because it avoids costly program delays which occur while Congress deliberates over additional funding. This saves the U.S. a lot of expenses.

Stassen went on to say an identical situation occurred in Turkey. The beginning of Turkey's jet air force started in the 1950 appropriations. That available money permitted boys, with very little mechanical ability, to be taken from the farms of Turkey and trained to be jet pilots in a four year course. The appropriated money created a repair shop, produced maintenance crews, and laid the foundation for a good jet air force (15: 504).

Hence, as Congress acted under Presidential orders to reduce spending, Stassen used these arguments to persuade Congress that unexpended funds carried over year to year in the Security Assistance Program were necessary and actually good for America.

In addition to the diminished Soviet threat and the Presidential influence to cut spending, there were world events impacting the creation of the Mutual Security Act of 1954. Two significant problems confronted the U.S. during 1954: finding a solution to the war in Indochina, and inducing the French and Italians to ratify the European Defense Community (EDC) treaty, which would open the door to West German rearmament (15: iii).

The problem facing America concerning the war in Indochina was how to keep France in the war and the U.S. out of it. The U.S. wanted to enthusiastically encourage France to battle the spread of Communism, but not appear too enthusiastic so as to demand the U.S. to commit ground forces to the cause. In the backwash of the Korean war, opposition on the home-front to any commitment of U.S. troops was too strong (15: iii).

EDC, the second problem facing the U.S. in 1954, was an ambitious, forward-looking program of military and political integration in Western Europe that was supposed to resolve the problem of how to get a German contribution to Western security without reviving the danger of an independent German military force and general staff.

Under EDC, German military contingents and those of other member-nations were to be welded together into a single "European" army, which would be subordinated to the political authority of the community as a whole. West Germany was to get the restoration of its national sovereignty, held in suspension by the Western powers since the war (15: v). If EDC failed to pass, the German divisions and material resources would continue to be withheld from the Western alliance. If German sovereignty was not restored, the government of pro-Western Adenauer, Chancellor of West Germany, might fall and West Germany turn into a neutral, or worse, an alliance of convenience with the East (15: vi). Consequently, the U.S. wanted France and Italy to ratify the treaty to bolster allied strength and security.

Therefore, as an introduction to the second major legislative act, the decline of the Soviet influence, the change of the leadership in the U.S. and Moscow, and the demands of two major world events were the important influences the U.S. legislators had to consider as they created the Mutual Security Assistance Act of 1954.

Primarily, the Mutual Security Act of 1954 did not create overwhelming new legislation. Instead, it was a consolidation of existing foreign aid statutes, a regrouping of all the old foreign assistance acts in an attempt to simplify the purpose and direction of U.S. foreign aid. It repealed all the old legislation and tried to make one bill out of them. It repealed some 14 pieces of legislation ranging from the Greek-Turkish program of 1947 to the Mutual Security Act of 1953 (15: 351). Because the majority of the Mutual Security Act of 1954 consisted of previously passed bills and previously authorized money, most of the material in the long bill was not controversial.

Military assistance under the 1954 act was furnished on a grant or loan basis. Overall, the Act authorized the President to expend

$1,270,000,000 - reduced from the $$1,430,300,000 originally slated for the Act (Executive Sessions of the Senate Foreign Relations Committee, 1954:887) - worth of equipment, materials, and services to foreign nations and international organizations to promote the foreign policy, security, and general welfare of the United States.

To combat the problems with EDC, legislators designed the Mutual Security Assistance Act of 1954 to explicitly authorize equipment and material to be delivered only to nations that signed and ratified the EDC treaty and joined together in developing collective defense programs in a manner satisfactory to the U.S. (15: 380). This was intended to encourage France and Italy to promptly ratify the treaty in order to gain assistance benefits. It was a valiant effort; however, EDC never came about. In the years after 1954, aid to foreign countries was conducted as usual.

The President was authorized to sell or enter into contracts for the procurement for sale of equipment, material, or services to any nation or international organization. The most significant change to security assistance legislation in 1954 occurred in the Act's section relating to the sale of military equipment. The act included a new, 3-year credit period for military sales. This meant nations did not have to initially pay large sums of cash, but could spread the costs of upgrading their military over a 3-year period. This gave the President great flexibility as long as the sale was consistent with the Charter of the United Nations. This 3-year credit period established the basis for Foreign Military Credit Sales (16: Appendix A).

The Act continued the United States' commitment to NATO by authorizing the President to make $780,000,000 worth of contributions to infrastructure programs of the North Atlantic Treaty Organization (22: 504).

According to Mr. Claxton, Staff Assistant to Assistant Secretary of State Morton, infrastructure was the underlying structural things that had to be built for the general NATO buildup, the largest part being airfields and the next largest pipelines to bring gasoline and oil to the airfields (15: 376-377).

The next most important authorization under the 1954 act was assistance to Europe. The United States' second highest security consideration in the world, behind North America, was the front-line region of Europe. Its location made it vital for forward basing of American defense materials. Although the Soviet threat had decreased, the U.S. maintained its commitment to NATO and to collective defense and authorized its largest amount of military assistance, $617,500,000, for Europe.

The Act also dealt with the Indochina War. Although President Eisenhower refused to commit troops to France's struggle with Indochina in early 1954, he did support the spread of Western-oriented governments in the region (24: 17). To encourage the stability of friendly states, the Mutual Security Act authorized $181,200,000 for the South Asian region and $583,600,000 for the Far East and the Pacific (22: 503-504).

In summary, the Mutual Security Act of 1954 was intended to combine all the old security assistance legislation into one new bill and was created under presidential pressure to reduce spending. Under these constraints, the act provided aid to NATO commitments, Europe's front-line defense, the ongoing war in Indochina, and the ratification of the EDC treaty.

Foreign Assistance Act of 1961. The next major piece of legislation considered is the Foreign Assistance Act of 1961. This act gave a new purpose and direction to the U.S. foreign assistance program by stressing long-term assistance. A brief history of security assistance's early years will show how the 1961 Act accomplished this redirection.

The first foreign-aid legislation, the Greek-Turkish Aid Bill and the Marshall Plan, *granted* large sums of money to countries vital to U.S. security interests. When the economies of these foreign countries grew strong enough to afford to pay for assistance and the United States needed to curtail its rate of spending on foreign assistance, Congress passed the Mutual Defense Act of 1949, creating the authority for Foreign Military Cash *Sales* to the foreign countries.

The next major change to security assistance came in 1954 when the Mutual Security Act allowed the foreign countries a 3-year credit period for repaying sales. This credit program laid the foundation for Foreign Military *Credit* Sales.

While the shift from grants, to sales, to credit sales was significant to the security assistance program, U.S. foreign aid remained a short-range program focusing usually one to four years ahead. One administration official stated. "we are tackling 20-year problems with 5-year plans, staffed with 2-year personnel working with 1-year appropriations" (27: 7).

The Foreign Assistance Act of 1961 changed all of this. It transformed U.S. foreign assistance from a short-range program into a long-range program. Where the Mutual Security Act of 1954 permitted a 3-year credit period, the Foreign Assistance Act of 1961 emphasized development loans repayable on manageable terms and conditions with emphasis on long-term financing (27: 1).

This switch to emphasizing long-term stemmed from the Committee on Foreign Relations' belief that foreign aid programs must be clearly related to the long-range goals of a recipient country. Many members of the Committee on Foreign Relations had experience with these foreign aid programs from the beginning of the security assistance. They had studied aid programs all over the world, issued reports of their findings, and authorized comprehensive studies of the problems of development. These experienced members pointed out that short-range cash grants rarely help a needy country. Instead of throwing foreign aid money at a country's problem under a "program", the committee perceived no amount of aid could materially improve a society whose leadership was not strongly committed to economic and social development. The committee believed previous U.S. programs were too heavily influenced by military considerations - direct "impact" programs, that often were short sighted (27: 7).

Departing from this short-range perspective, the Foreign Assistance Act of 1961 stressed the underlying principle of continuity. Aid programs were supposed to respond to the efforts of the foreign peoples to help themselves and future assistance would follow this principle.

All loans extended under the new authority permitted up to 50 years to repay, with interest rates as low as 1 percent and in some cases with no repayment of principal for initial periods up to 10 years. To accomplish this, the Act authorized the President to borrow $8.787 billion ($1,187 billion in fiscal year 1962 and $1.9 billion in each of the following 4 fiscal years) to finance the new development loans (27: 10).

The Committee on Foreign Relations believed the long-term borrowing authority to be the most important part of the act (27: 10). Since most poor countries did not need and could not absorb large amounts of aid at one time, the long-term borrowing promoted efficiency, economy, and durable economic growth (27: 12).

The Act authorized almost $1.1 billion for defense support and assistance to 37 countries, $500 million to be used in 1961 and $581 million for 1962 (27:21). While many NATO countries still received aid, most of the assistance went to Greece, Turkey, Pakistan, Korea, and Vietnam (27:22).

The Act provided a 2-year authorization for military assistance programs totalling $1.8 billion (27:24). As in previous legislation, military assistance could be furnished in terms and conditions determined by the President and to any country. Assistance could be provided through defense articles or services acquired from any source by loan, lease, sale, exchange, grant, or any other means (27:24). Therefore, the Foreign Assistance Act of 1961 encouraged long-term assistance through standard means.

Foreign Military Sales Act of 1968. By 1968 the United States was deeply involved with the war in Southeast Asia and struggling with the ever-growing problems related to the antiwar opposition. President Lyndon Johnson was determined to maintain the present level of foreign aid in spite of the growing resistance he faced from Congress. The country's involvement in Vietnam contributed significantly to the growing problem of the balance-of-payments deficit. Several respected economists put the annual costs for the U.S. involvement from 1964 to 1967 at $1.6 billion which accounts primarily for increases in military spending overseas (12: 89). In a May 18, 1966 press conference, then Treasury Secretary, Henry

Fowler remarked, " We suggest that careful analysis will support the proposition that, absent the Vietnam build-up, the United States might have moved substantially closer to equilibrium in its balance of payments" (12: 91). The congressional leaders that once supported Johnson and his foreign policy initiatives had become increasingly hostile as a result of the Administration's escalation of our involvement in Vietnam.

It should be noted that from the period of 1966 to 1975 the grant aid funding that was supplied to support Southeast Asia was part of the regular Department of Defense appropriation. This funding was called military assistance service funded or MASF. The money was used to provide military equipment, services, and training to countries that were involved in the conflict in Southeast Asia (14: 106).

In 1965, President Johnson had no problem getting Congressional approval for $3.25 billion in foreign aid (12: 84). The President had purposely scaled down his request from $3.6 billion to avoid any opposition from Congress and the tactic worked. Plus, the threat of Communism remained and the need to ensure both national and international security was still considered an important part of American foreign policy.

The Foreign Military Sales Act of 1968, was designed to revise and consolidate all of the foreign assistance legislation related to military exports (29: 1320). The Act authorized sales by the United States to friendly foreign countries that had enough resources and wealth to maintain their own military forces or at least assume the majority of this responsibility without placing an unreasonable strain on the economy of the nation as a whole (29: 1321). It was further stated that sales would be approved only if they were consistent with existing American foreign policy practices and interests. The

Act also set down the following additional guidelines for eligibility and the purposes for which sales would be authorized.

In regard to eligibility, the sale of defense articles or services to a country had to contribute to the security of the United States and promote world peace for the sale to be approved. The receiving organization or country was required to agree not to transfer the articles to any other person(s) or nation without the prior approval of the United States. And finally, the Act stipulated that services/articles would not be sold to any country which seized or imposed fines on an American fishing vessel while it was fishing in international waters or twelve miles from the coast of that country (29: 1322).

The purposes for which sales could be authorized were also clearly outlined in the Act. The United States would sell defense articles/services only to friendly nations for the purpose of internal security, self-defense, or to allow participation in United Nations authorized activities. The items or services could be used by the friendly country's military forces to construct public projects that contributed to the economic or social development of the country, although this should not be the sole function of that country's military forces; but, the civic projects should not detract from the military mission (29: 1323). These purposes were authorized with the added provision that none of the funds included in the agreement could be used to extend or guarantee credit on the sale of weapons systems such as missiles or aircraft used for military purposes, to any underdeveloped countries other than those already established as important to U.S. security interests. These established countries included Turkey, Iran, the Philippines, Greece, the Republic of China, Israel, and Korea. The President could waive this if it was determined to be in the best interest of the national security of the United States (29: 1323).

The Act divided foreign military sales into two separate categories: cash and credit. For cash sales, the President could sell defense articles from the inventory of the Department of Defense and defense services to any friendly country or international organization. In return, the recipients agreed to pay no less than the value of the item or services in United States dollars. Payment was to be made in advance unless the President decided to allow for a reasonable period of repayment, which was not to exceed 120 days. This was done only if the President felt that this sale and grace-period authorization was in the best interest of the United States (29: 1323).

The Act also provided authorization for the President to enter into contracts to procure items for sale to other countries provided the receiving country or organization illustrated a commitment to make payment in full or set aside funds to make the required payments within 120 days of the delivery of the items or services. The President could enter into contracts with fixed prices for the articles or services when he determined such contracts to be in the best interest of the United States (29: 1323).

For credit sales, the President could authorize the finance of the purchase of defense articles and services by friendly countries or organizations in terms of repayment that were to be made to the United States within a period not to exceed ten years after the delivery of the articles or services provided (29: 1324). The President could use his power to guarantee any individual or private business against the possible credit risks of a failure to pay by any of these countries. This protected these individuals and private businesses against any financial losses they might incur as a result of their financing sales to foreign countries (29: 1324).

The Act also outlined the amounts to be authorized and the limits or ceilings on those authorizations for some regional areas. In the area of export controls, for the year 1969, the President was authorized a total of $269,000,000 for the purpose of foreign military sales credits. The total amount of military assistance pursuant to the Foreign Assistance Act of 1961, as amended, of cash sales excluding training, was not to exceed $75,000,000 for the Latin American countries in 1969. The total for the African countries under the same guidelines and for the same fiscal year was not to exceed $40,000,000. The President was authorized to waive these limitations if he felt it was in the best interest of the security of the United States. Also, if it was determined that any economically underdeveloped countries were diverting assistance to unnecessary military programs and hindering that country's social and economic well-being, then they could be excluded from eligibility for further assistance (29: 1324-1325). The Foreign Military Sales Act was approved on October 22, 1968 and, as mentioned earlier, was designed to consolidate and revise foreign assistance legislation regarding reimbursable military exports.

The next significant legislative enactment used to bring about changes in foreign military sales legislation was the International Security Assistance and Arms Export Control Act of 1976.

International Security Assistance and Arms Export Control Act of 1976. By 1976 the United States had withdrawn from Vietnam and, as a result of this controversial war, had made changes to its foreign policy. The

Nixon Doctrine had proclaimed that the U.S. would continue to help friendly nations in their efforts to deter aggression but only when we were asked to and only if the nation requesting assistance was willing to fight on its own behalf (20: 235). For the past decade, the U.S. had supplied the vast majority of all weapons distributed throughout the world. From 1966 to 1976, the United States had exported as many weapons as the rest of the world combined (20: 243). The International Security Assistance and Arms Export Control Act was used to amend the Foreign Assistance Act of 1961 and to create the Arms Export Control Act (AECA). These changes consolidated all existing legislation that pertained to arms sales and helped regulate the amount of arms exported. The Act called for the gradual phase out of the Military Assistance Program (MAP) and included provisions for the International Military and Education program, thus separating it from MAP. At the time, congressional leaders were concerned over the large amount of weapons being exported by the U.S. and used this legislation as a means of checking the President's ability to sell arms at will (20: 244-245).

The Act reflected a shift in policy geared towards changing from a mode of selling arms to maintaining more control over arms sales. It allowed Congress to retain the right to veto proposed arms sales. This veto power was granted in the Nelson amendment to the FY 1975 foreign aid authorization bill. In addition, it extended the period of time allowed to veto from twenty to thirty days (21: 9-10). This congressional review of sales could be waived by the president if he felt an emergency existed which threatened the national security of the United States.

Specifically, the Act authorized the President $196,700,000 for military assistance during fiscal year 1976 and $177,300,000 for fiscal year

1977. In addition, it limited the number of countries that could be supported under the MAP to twenty in 1976 and decreased that number to twelve in 1977 (30: 729). The decreasing dollar amounts and numbers of countries authorized annually clearly indicated the gradual reduction or phasing out of MAP mentioned earlier.

The Act contained a number of changes which are designed to limit the power of the president and give Congress more influence in shaping foreign policy decisions. In the area of defense stockpiling, the Act stipulates that no defense article that has been set aside for a foreign government may be released to that government without authorization from Congress. It also states that after September of 1977, Congress must approve all military assistance advisory groups, missions, or any other organization of U.S. armed forces personnel deployed to carry out advisory duties. The number of these advisory groups was also limited to 34 (30: 730-731). Under the area of arms exports, the Act points out that the President should initiate multilateral discussions with all principal arms suppliers in order to limit the number of arms transfers in the interest of world peace. It requires the President to conduct a thorough study of the United States' arms sales policies to examine the benefits and rationale behind our programs and submit a report of the findings to Congress. The President is restricted from approving the transfer of defense articles unless he has submitted a written proposal to the House Speaker and the Committee on Foreign Relations requesting such a transfer thirty days prior (30: 734-735).

The Act included an amendment to the Foreign Military Sales Act which gives the President the power to control the import and export of all defense articles. The President was authorized to designate exactly what is and is not considered to be a defense article. This control over the licensing of importers and exporters was done in the interest of promoting world peace and to further the security and foreign policies of the United States. This amendment also repealed sections of the Mutual Security Act of 1954 that referenced or pertained to arms export and control (30: 744).

Significantly, the legislation set guidelines for U.S. policy on countries accused or suspected of human rights violations. It stipulated that the United States should work to promote respect for human rights and individual freedoms and specifically stated,

> It is further the policy of the United States that, except under circumstances specified in this section, no security assistance may be provided to any country the government of which engages in a consistent pattern of gross violations of internationally recognized human rights (30: 748).

The Act established the position of Coordinator for Human Rights and Humanitarian Affairs. The Coordinator was appointed by the President and reported to the Secretary of State on all matters regarding human rights and humanitarian issues (30: 750). The Secretary of State was required to provide Congress with a report on the observance of human rights policy by any countries who were requesting or being considered for security assistance.

Conflicts of interest between the new guidelines and U.S. foreign policy can be observed in the Congressional records of the hearings on the International Security Assistance and Arms Export Control Act. The subject of human rights violations is addressed on numerous occasions. The Honorable Donald M. Fraser, a member of the International Relations

Committee, expressed his concern over the problems being experienced in South Korea during this time. President Park of Korea had arrested a group of rival political leaders for no apparent reason other than political convenience. In spite of these violations, we were continuing our economic and military support to South Korea. This was clearly a case where the United States did not approve of the actions of another government, but in the interest of national security and deterrence of Communist aggression, continued to support the government in question (17: 14-16). Former Secretary of State Henry Kissinger, during these same hearings remarked,

> We have strongly made known our views to the Korean government and there should be no doubt about the concern of the U.S. on the human rights issue. At the same time we cannot lose sight of our basic concerns over the security situation on the Korean peninsula and its importance to the peace and security of the area. Our request is based on our own assessment of the need to maintain the military balance in Korea and is in support of our security objectives in Korea, Japan, and East Asia generally (17: 71).

Another amendment to the Foreign Assistance Act of 1961 prohibited the United States from rendering assistance to any countries that provided refuge or sanctuary to international terrorists. This could be waived by the President if it was believed to be in the best interest of the national security of the United States (30: 753).

Finally, the Act specifies economic assistance by country or region. The Middle East policy was determined by the circumstances and events of the time. Congress saw the civil unrest in Lebanon as a threat to the security and peace in that region of the world. An additional $20,000,000 was set aside to help in the relief effort there. The refugees of Cyprus were given $10,000,000 more than they received under the Foreign Assistance Act of

1961, for a total of $40,000,000. Assistance to Turkey, totaling no more than $125,000,000 for fiscal year 1977, was contingent upon Turkey's continued adherence to the cease-fire and an end to the Turkish build-up of forces on Cyprus. The Act stated that no assistance would be granted to any nation, organization, or individual for the purpose of conducting or promoting, either directly or indirectly, any type of military or paramilitary operations in the country of Angola. Congress used this section of the Act and the following one to express their disapproval of the Soviet Union's involvement in Angola during this time. The South American country of Chile was also affected by this new legislation. Chile was guilty of violations of internationally recognized human rights and as a result there would be no security assistance, military training or education granted to them as of the date of this enactment. They would be allowed a total of $27,500,000 for economic assistance with a provision for an additional $27,500,000 if the government of Chile did not engage in a consistent pattern of human rights violations. The International Security Assistance and Arms Export Control Act was approved on June 30, 1976.

International Security Assistance Act of 1979. The Carter administration furthered the new attitudes and policies of restraint established in the International Security Assistance and Arms Export Control Act of 1976. In May of 1977, President Carter made it clear that under his administration, conventional arms transfers would be used as the exception in foreign policy practices and only when it could be clearly shown to be significant in contributing to the security interests of the United States (21: 10). Carter's policy followed the changes introduced in the International

Security Assistance and Arms Export Control Act of 1976. He planned to continue the effort to promote the human rights issue and to consider the impact of U.S. economic assistance to receiving countries. Multilateral negotiations were to be used to reduce international arms transfers and the United S' ites would reduce the dollar amount of commitments made in the area of arms transfers. The ceiling for 1978 was set at $8.4 billion, which was an eight percent decrease from 1977 (21: 11).

A number of factors affected the administration's stand on foreign policy. During this period, the United States was still very concerned with the growing power of the Soviet Union. Negotiations were in progress for the Strategic Arms Limitations Talks, SALT II treaty. This agreement would include a test ban against nuclear explosives, reduce the transfer of arms to other countries, prohibit attacks on space satellites, and place limitations on the number of forces deployed in the Indian Ocean. The President described the U.S. relationship with the Soviet Union as competitive. In an address to Naval Academy graduates he summed up his position by saying, "The Soviet Union can choose either confrontation or cooperation. The United States is adequately prepared to meet either choice" (9: 14).

The Soviet Union continued its efforts to spread Communism through indirect support of its satellites. In Africa, the Cuban government had more than 20,000 troops deployed to the country of Angola and had trained Katangans there who were responsible for a recent uprising in the country of Zaire (10: 6). Just three months earlier, President Carter had authorized an extension of credit to Zaire of $17,500,000 in an effort to help that country's failing economy and government (9: 35). Cuban and Soviet involvement did nothing more than throw fuel on the fire.

The United States continued to show a growing interest in the increasingly unstable Middle East. In September of 1978, Egyptian President Sadat and Israeli Prime Minister Begin met with President Carter at Camp David to set up a framework for peace in the Middle East. The Shah of Iran, after years of United States support and amidst great civil unrest and disturbances, left his country in January of 1979 and the government of our former ally was taken over by the Ayatollah Khomeini, a radical religious leader (11: 3).

In August, 1978, Turkey and Greece, the countries where U.S. foreign assistance has its roots, were receiving attention from the United States government again. Four years earlier, the Turkish government had invaded the Greek island of Cyprus, using U.S. provided equipment. As a result, an arms embargo had been placed on Turkey and the country had been receiving no United States support. However, fears of Soviet intervention and the lack of beneficial results caused the U.S. to take a second look at the sanctions imposed (10: 7).

The International Security Assistance Act of 1979 reflected many of the concerns and policy guidelines set down by the President and called for by the events of the time in the provisions it made. In the area of human rights the Act stated,

> In allocating the funds authorized to be appropriated by this Act and the Arms Export Control Act, the President shall take into account significant improvements in the human rights records of recipient countries, except that such allocations may not contravene any other provisions of law (31: 702).

This was clearly a continuation of the standards set down in the International Security Assistance and Arms Export Control Act of 1976.

In the economic support fund, the Act amended the previous year's limit of $1,902,000,000 by increasing the amount available for fiscal year 1980 to $1,935,000,000. The peace efforts in the Middle East were supported by authorizations of $785,000,000 and $750,000,000 for Israel and Egypt, respectively. Not less than two-thirds of these amounts were to be provided on a grant basis. The fund also made available $68,000,000 for the countries of southern Africa to assist in refugee support and economic assistance. The Act prohibited any assistance to those countries seen as instigators in the conflicts of that region. These included, Angola, Zambia, Tanzania and Mozambique. Refugee relief and reconciliation efforts on the island of Cyprus were authorized $15,000,000 for fiscal year 1980. In spite of Turkey's invasion of Cyprus, three years earlier, the U.S. continued to provide support to Turkey in hopes of promoting economic and political stability within the country. Turkey was authorized not more than $98,000,000 for fiscal year 1980 and an additional $100,000,000 for fiscal year 1979. Congress stated that it remained the policy of the United States that all foreign troops should be removed from Cyprus (31: 703-711).

Finally, the Act included an authorization for the International Military Education and Training Program which matched the previous year's amount of $31,800,000 (31: 705). In addition, it initiated a reduction in the amount authorized to support peace-keeping operations. There was a total of $30,900,000 authorized for fiscal year 1979 and only $21,100,000 for 1980. The International Security Assistance Act of 1979 was approved on October 29, 1979.

The Reagan Administration Policies. The Reagan Administration brought major changes to U.S. security assistance. President Reagan steamrolled into office with a firm plan to increase America's military strength, including strengthening security measures accomplished through foreign assistance. Due to President Reagan's goals, the Security Assistance Program received greater funding and boosted economic support to foreign recipients.

The change from President Carter to President Reagan in January 1981 brought widespread changes to the U.S. Defense Department and the Security Assistance Program. President Reagan aggressively pushed for building U.S. defense. In his State of the Union address on February 18, President Reagan told the American people "since 1970, the Soviet Union has invested $300 billion more in its military forces than the U.S. As a result of this massive build-up, the Soviets have made a significant numerical advantage" (23: i). He continued his point in a speech at West Point in May when he said "treaties are no substitute for arms buildup" (13: 720).

President Reagan backed his position with action as well. Less than one month after election, he announced his plan to increase the military budget from 24.1 percent of federal spending in FY81 to 32.1 percent in FY84 and have a $33 billion increase in the defense budgets for FY81 and FY82 (23: i). As expected, these increases in defense spilled over into the Security Assistance Program.

With President Reagan's enthusiasm for defense buildup, more money poured into the U.S. Security Assistance Program. Just two months after being elected, President Reagan sought $6.9 billion for security assistance in FY82, $900 million over former President Carter's request

(13: 719). In fact, during President Reagan's first term, the administration and Congress worked together to accomplish two main objectives, 1) to increase security assistance funding levels, and 2) to balance military assistance with economic aid programs (3: 23).

President Reagan's Administration primarily determined to increase the funding for security assistance due to the presence of three threats: Soviet military expansion, Soviet influence in Afghanistan, and the Soviet threat to Poland. As President Reagan stated, he believed the Soviet Union had spent $300 billion more on defense than the U.S. and he wanted more U.S. funding to decrease the gap between the Soviet military and that of the U.S.

In addition to the Soviet military strength, President Reagan had two Soviet threats that supported his campaign for increased funding. The Soviet's invasion of Afghanistan, which started during Carter's Administration in 1979, continued to threaten the stability of that region. Also, the Soviets threatened to invade Poland to suppress Poland's trade union, Solidarity, which was protesting to obtain a 5-day work week (13: 730). The leaders of the Soviet Union agreed the defiance of Solidarity concerned the entire Soviet bloc and hinted at invading Poland to squash the worker's trade union (13: 730).

President Reagan also discovered limited funding seriously restricted the application of security assistance (3: 24). His Administration soon corrected that problem. Under President Reagan, overall funding for security assistance grew by 84 percent from FY 1981 to FY 1986 and IMET funding increased from $28.4 million in FY 1981 to $54.5 million in FY 1986 (3: 24).

When the Reagan Administration took office, the United States had no effective policies, backed by economic and military assistance programs, to counter a near disastrous situation in Central America (3: 24). Rebel insurgency forces in El Salvador were slaying thousands of people and the State Department determined the Soviets were supplying arms to the rebels through Cuba and Nicaragua (13: 748). Responding to the imminent crisis, the President's National Bipartisan Commission on Central America concluded that U.S. interests "require a significantly larger program of military assistance, as well as greatly expanded support for economic growth and social reform" (2: 1).

Mainly due to this crisis, Congress and the Administration recognized that healthy growing economies were fundamental to political and economic reform in the Third World. In those countries fighting insurgencies, sound economic management is, in fact, as important as military capability. As a result, budget authority for the Economic Support Fund (ESF) and direct assistance was increased in step with military assistance (3: 24). With more emphasis on the ESF, the number of countries receiving ESF went from 28 to 44 under Reagan's administration (3: 26).

Although there was no benchmark security assistance legislation passed during President Reagan's two terms, his Administration impacted two key areas of the Security Assistance Program. The Reagan Administration worked hard to 1) increase security assistance funding and 2) to increase economic aid.

Conclusion

This chapter reviewed major foreign assistance legislation from 1947 through 1988. It concentrated on the most significant aspects of each legislative act in an attempt to capture the factors that have shaped the Security Assistance Program. Chapter four will consolidate and compare these factors for analysis.

IV. Analysis

Introduction

This chapter conducts an analysis of the information gathered in the literature review. It compares three categories of findings, 1) the attitudes and policies of the present leadership, 2) the significant authorizations of each legislative act, and 3) the influence of global events on security assistance spending.

Greek-Turkish Aid Bill

President Truman began U.S. security assistance by initiating a departure from isolationism in the Truman Doctrine. The outcome was the Greek-Turkish Aid Bill which provided $400 million of assistance to Greece and Turkey to combat Soviet expansion.

Mutual Defense Act of 1949

Through this Act, Truman continued his dedication to collective defense by increasing alliances, treaties, and contracts. Authorizations also significantly increased with $1 billion authorized to countries of the NATO alliance. These large increases were needed to combat the Soviet military buildup in Germany, the Soviet blockade of Berlin, and the Communist threat to Asia.

Mutual Security Act of 1954

When President Eisenhower entered office, he reversed Truman's trend of increased spending on security assistance. In fact, Eisenhower demanded curtailment of military spending. Authorizations to NATO fell to $780 million. Eisenhower could decrease spending because the new Soviet leadership seemed less threatening than the previous regime; plus, the U.S. was still not fully involved in the Indochina War.

Foreign Assistance Act of 1961

In 1961, the United States made an extreme transition in foreign assistance. They shifted from a policy of throwing short-term, "program" money towards U.S. security concerns to making long-term foreign aid solutions. Because of this, the President was authorized over $8 billion for long-term assistance. At the same time, major powers such as Japan and Europe began to help improve the underdeveloped countries of the world (27: 4).

Foreign Military Sales Act of 1968

In 1968, President Johnson maintained the present the level of security assistance even though Congress urged a reduction in overseas spending. America's costly involvement in the Vietnam War and the growing opposition to additional spending were critical in shaping the policies of this time period. As a result of these influences, exports in foreign military sales were limited to $269,000,000.

International Security Assistance and Arms Export Control Act of 1976

This legislation continued a tight control on security assistance spending. Congress was deeply concerned over the amount of arms being exported and began limiting the President's authority to sell arms. Authorizations continued to decline with only $196,700,000 for military assistance. The United States was involved in no major conflicts at this time and, with the war in Southeast Asia over, conditions were conducive to decreased spending.

The International Security Assistance Act of 1979

The Carter Administration continued to promote decreased spending through the reduction of arms transfers. Authorizations remained relatively small with $785 million to Israel; $750 million to Egypt; and $68 million to Southern Africa. Both the overthrow of the Shah of Iran and the presence of Cuban troops in Angola were causes for concern, but the driving force behind the policies of the Carter Administration was the Middle East peace effort.

The Reagan Administration Policies

President Reagan reversed the years of low defense spending. His Administration raised the budget for security assistance to $6.9 billion, $900 million above Carter's provision. The massive Soviet buildup in the 1970s, the Soviet expansion into Afghanistan, the Soviet threat to invade Poland, and the disastrous situation in Central America supported Reagan's desire for strengthening U.S. defense.

Conclusion

An indication of what shapes the Security Assistance Program cannot be ascertained from comparing the authorization figures of this literature review. The figures found in the legislative acts sometimes specify the amounts spent on military assistance, sometimes amounts for the entire security assistance program, and other times for several categories mixed together.

Analysis of the influence of global events does reveal factors that shape the Security Assistance Program. At the beginning of the program in 1947, U.S. security assistance was devoted solely to Greece and Turkey to prevent Soviet expansion. When the free nations of the world realized no individual country could withstand Soviet expansion, the U.S. began directing its security assistance into building alliances and treaties such as NATO under the 1949 Act. After these alliances were established, the U.S. applied its security assistance dollars to specific geographic locations threatened by Communism. The last four legislative acts verify this because security assistance was increased to certain geographic locations, e.g. Vietnam, Lebanon, the Middle East, and Afghanistan. Therefore, global events do impact where the United States provides assistance.

Analysis also reveals a relationship between the attitudes and policies of the present leadership and the shaping of the Security Assistance Program. Prior to the Greek-Turkish Aid Bill, the United States' attitude of isolationism caused limited security assistance. When President Truman committed to containing Soviet expansion, he set the course for U.S. security assistance. For the next seven years, President Truman consistently increased security assistance spending. However, President Eisenhower's

Administration reversed Truman's spending trend by demanding defense spending cuts. This idea of reduced spending continued until the beginning of the Vietnam War when President Johnson stressed maintaining the present security assistance budget. Maintaining the status quo was unhindered during Johnson's tenure and on through the Carter Administration. Then, when President Reagan took office, his Administration reversed the stagnant defense spending of the last two decades by demanding substantial increases in defense and security assistance for the next eight years.

In answering the research question, "What factors shape the direction of the Security Assistance Program?", research concludes there are three main factors influencing the direction of the program. The Soviet threat has always been the primary reason for security assistance. Communism threatened Greece and Turkey, caused the creation of NATO, and forced U.S. involvement in various trouble spots in the world.

Secondly, global events shape the direction of the Security Assistance Program. Problems such as the Soviet buildup in Germany, the fall of China to Mao Tse-tung, the war in Vietnam, and the conflict in the Middle East significantly influenced the size and direction of security assistance spending at the time.

Lastly, the attitudes and policies of the current leadership shape the direction of the Security Assistance Program. President Truman began a departure from isolationism by promoting assistance to Greece and Turkey and by seeking treaties and alliances. However, each subsequent administration promoted its own unique ideas about security assistance. Eisenhower demanded spending cuts, Johnson vowed to maintain current levels of support, and President Reagan launched aggressive increases in defense and security assistance spending.

In conclusion, this thesis determined that the threat of Communism, the attitudes and policies of the current leadership, and the impact of global events were the main factors that shape the direction of the Security Assistance Program.

Bibliography

1. Borklund, Carl W. U.S. Defense and Military Fact Book. Santa Barbara: ABC-CLIO, Inc., 1991.

2. Congressional Presentation for Security Assistance Programs, FY 1985. Washington: GPO, 1985.

3. Congressional Presentation for Security Assistance Programs, FY 1987, Volume 1. Washington: GPO, 1987.

4. Congressional Presentation for Security Assistance Programs, FY 1994, Washington: GPO, 1993.

5. Cooper, Donald R. and C. William Emory. Business Research Methods. Boston: Irwin, 1991.

6. Curti, Merle and Lewis P. Todd. Rise of the American Nation. New York: Harcourt, Brace & World, Inc., 1969.

7. Department of State. A Decade of American Foreign Policy. Basic Documents, 1941-49. Washington: GPO, 1950.

8. Department of State. Foreign Relations of the United States. Department of State Publication 8592, Vol. V., 1947. Washington: GPO, 1971.

9. Department of State Bulletin. Volume 78, Number 2016. Washington: GPO, July 1978.

10. Department of State Bulletin. Volume 78, Number 2017. Washington: GPO, August 1978.

11. Department of State Bulletin. Volume 79, Number 2023. Washington: GPO, February 1979.

12. Divine, Robert A. The Johnson Years, Volume Two - Vietnam, the Environment, and Science. Lawrence: University Press of Kansas, 1987.

13. Elaine, P. A. Chronology 1981. Foreign Affairs, Volume 60, Number 3. New York: Council on Foreign Relations, Inc., 1982.

14. Foreign Military Sales, Foreign Military Construction Sales and Military Assistance Facts, Washington: Data Management Division, Comptroller, DSAA, 1990.

15. Foreign Relations Committee. Executive Sessions of the Senate Foreign Relations Committee. Volume 6, 83rd Congress, 2nd Session, 1954. Washington: GPO, 1977.

16. Graves, Ernest and Steven A. Hildreth. U.S. Security Assistance, The Political Process. Lexington MA: D.C. Heath and Co., 1985.

17. House of Representatives. Hearings Before the Committee on International Relations. Hearing, 94th Congress, 2nd Session, 1976. Washington: GPO, 1976.

18. House of Representatives. Miscellaneous Reports Volume 6. Washington: GPO, 1949.

19. Hovey, Harold A. United States Military Assistance, A Study of Policies and Practices. New York: Frederick A. Praeger Publishers, 1965.

20. Joiner, Harry M. American Foreign Policy, The Kissinger Era. Huntsville AL: The Strode Publishers, Inc., 1977.

21. Labrie, Roger P. and others. U.S. Arms Sales Policy Background and Issues. Washington: American Enterprise Institute for Public Policy Research, 1982.

22. Mutual Security Program, Part 4. Washington: GPO, 1980.

23. The Reagan Defense Market. Greenwich CT: DMS Inc., 1981.

24. Record, Jeffrey. Revising U.S. Military Strategy, Tailoring Means to Ends. McLean VA: Pergamon-Brassey's International Defense Publishers, 1984.

25. Semmell, Andrew K. "Security Assistance: U.S. and Soviet Patterns," in Foreign Policy: U.S.A./U.S.S.R. Beverly Hills: Sage Publishing Company, 1982.

26. Senate Miscellaneous Reports Volume 4. Washington: GPO, 1949.

27. Senate Miscellaneous Reports on Public Bills, Volume 4. Washington: GPO, 1961.

28. Truman, Harry S. Memoirs by Harry S. Truman. Garden City NY: Doubleday & Company, 1956.

29. United States At Large, Laws and Current Resolutions Enacted During the Second Session of the Ninetieth Congress of the United States of America, 1968, Volume 82. Washington: GPO, 1969.

30. United States Congre. , International Security Assistance and Arms Export Control Act of 1976. Public Law 94-329. Washington: GPO, 1978.

31. United States Congress. International Security Assistance Act of 1979. Public Law 96-92. Washington: GPO, 1979.

32. Weigley, Russell F. The American Way of War, A History of United States Military Strategy and Policy. Bloomington: Indiana University Press, 1977.